AF211917

CAL GODFREY

LAWN GEEK

The Ultimate Guide to Lawn Care, Discover the Professional Tricks and Useful Tips on How to Care For Your Own Lawn

Descrierea CIP a Bibliotecii Naţionale a României
CAL GODFREY
   LAWN GEEK. The Ultimate Guide to Lawn Care, Discover the Professional Tricks and Useful Tips on How to Care For Your Own Lawn / Cal Godfrey – Bucharest: Editura My Ebook, 2021
   ISBN

CAL GODFREY

LAWN GEEK

The Ultimate Guide to Lawn Care, Discover the Professional Tricks and Useful Tips on How to Care For Your Own Lawn

My Ebook Publishing House
Bucharest, 2021

TABLE OF CONTENTS

INTRODUCTION

Men have had fights over it. It's a battle of suburbia that has yet to be won. They all compete for the coveted prize with the best machines made by man. Lawn care has actually become a competition these days. Do you want a lawn to make your neighbors jealous for?

Lawns, yard, and grass: everyone has a name for that green space, but what it really is, is your own little piece of the earth. You own it, you take care of it, and you're responsible for it. It needs you! And, you need it.

Our lawns have become a major player in our eco-system, after all it covers about 50 million acres in just America (2003 estimate).

That means what you do is multiplied thousands of times over, every day in our country. So it's important that you do things right and stop flying by the seat of your pants just because that's the way you've always done it.

Besides keeping your house from sinking into some dark abyss, your lawn is an important part of our environment. Environmentally, turf grass reduces carbon dioxide emissions, mitigating the heat island effect commonly found in our urban environments.

Lawns also reduce energy consumption through its cooling effects and contribute to efforts to reduce global warming trends. Grass reduces soil erosion by holding the soil in place during heavy flooding. Just 2,500 square feet of lawn not only absorbs carbon dioxide from the air, but it also releases enough oxygen for a family of four to breathe.

It can say volumes about your pride as a homeowner. It can say volumes about your lack of pride as a homeowner.

The truth is that if you live in a community that thrives on the way houses look – ala Stepford – then lawn care is important to you!

But what the experts say is true: grass and lawns are an important part of the environment. Let's face it: your turf grass, lawn, yard, or whatever you want to call it, is pretty cool. Not only does grass smell good when you mow it, but grass feels good to walk across. My kids like playing on it, and my dogs definitely like it for entirely different reasons. Grass looks pretty in the early morning with the dew sparkling across it, or in the fall when the first frost settles in.

The only thing all that lovely lawn of green grass asks is a little care, a little patience, and to be fed and groomed occasionally. Pretty much what your kids expect, except you'll never have to set up a college fund for your grass.

Believe it or not, some people feel that a beautifully manicured lawn is a hazard to the environment. They feel they are unhealthy habitats that consume not only time, but also precious resources

In actuality, a well manicured and well taken care of lawn can actually be a thriving eco-system that can help all sorts of living things thrive and grow. But this book isn't really about that part of keeping a great lawn.

What we hope to do in this book is to help you realize your dream of having a beautifully manicured lawn by using the techniques and tricks that are used by professional landscapers.

Many times, there are people who believe that having a beautiful lawn requires the use of harmful fertilizers and other components that can damage the environment. The reality is that you can have a beautiful lawn without harming the environment.

Once you learn all of the particulars, we're pretty sure that you'll be amazed how you can achieve a beautiful front yard,

11

back yard, and side yard – a beautiful lawn that your neighbors will be envious of.

What do you really need? Well, we're going to show you. How do you take care of it? We'll show you that too.

You can have a beautiful lawn and get rid of all the critiques from those natural people. There are many, many ways to cultivate and take care of your lawn without compromising on environmental concerns or taking up a bunch of your time.

Experts agree that a great lawn can be a reality. How do you achieve that? Read on, dear friend, read on!

STARTING FROM SCRATCH

Just because it's easier, let's assume that you have no grass at all or that your grass is mostly dead and you need to start from square one. There are many, many people out there who have had their homes built and now are faced with a patch of dirt where grass should be.

If you're like me, however, you may already have a lawn, but there are many, many dead patches all around the yard that need worked on. Well, we can work on that as well!

All you need to start with is a little grass seed and a little know how!

There are literally hundreds of grass seeds to choose from when you are trying to figure out what you want your yard to look like. Believe it or not, all of these various grasses can make your lawn look a different way.

What we're trying to say is that grass isn't just grass. There are different colors of green, different ways the grass lays, different ways the grass grows. Depending on what you're looking for, choosing the right grass for your lifestyle and preference can make all the difference in having a lawn you can be proud of.

The first thing you need to do before choosing a grass seed is to prepare the land. If you have a bare patch of land, all that entails is to till up the area until you have a fine powder of dirt. Then till that area again until the powder is even more powdery. Then you can be assured you have a great place for your grass to grow!

What do you do, though, if you have patches that need to be filled in? Actually, you need to do much the same thing. Till up each piece of land until you have a very fine powder to work with.

In either situation, once you have the land tilled up, you'll need to add in a little bit of fertilizer to make the ground more receptive to the seed it will be receiving. We'll address specific fertilizers a little bit later, but you need to find one that will help you achieve your desired results.

Alright, you've got the ground prepared. Now what do you put in it?

GRASS VARIETIES

You can't just go to your local home improvement store and tell the clerk you need some grass seed. Sorry, but the process is much more involved than that!

How will you know which grass seed you need? Here are just a few varieties. How would you make the choice?

Fescue Bahia Bluegrass Bermuda Zoysia Bent Grass Centipede St. Augustine

And that's just a few of the varieties out there. Would you know which one you'd want to adorn your yard? Well, certainly not without a little information!

As we said before, there are literally hundreds of different varieties out there. How do you know which one is right for you? Well, we can't choose your grass seed, but we can tell you the attributes of different varieties, and then you can choose for yourself!

First, though, consider what you're looking for when it comes to your lawn and how to care for it. Are you wondering which grass is best for you? Here are a few considerations:

❑ **Maintenance required:** some grass species require more care than other, high maintenance grasses.

❑ **Climate conditions:** most grasses have a preference for specific climates such as humid, coastal, dry, and cool.

❑ **Temperature tolerance:** each grass performs better or worse depending on the average temperature range during the growing season.

- **Drought resistance:** some grass species are better suited quickly recover after going dormant during extended drought conditions.

- **Shade adaptation:** grass species are classified by how much or how little sunlight they need to maintain their health and vigor.

❑ **Wear resistance:** this is a measurement of how well a grass species can recover from foot traffic.

Not every grass is good for every climate. Some species are good for shade, others are good for cold climates and still others perform better in extremely hot areas. The following is a list of the best readily available grasses for specific adaptations.

Best for shady areas

Fine-leaf Fescue: (cool season) does not tolerate traffic, drought resistant, shade tolerant. Some varieties are more disease resistant.

Tall Fescue: (transition zone) low maintenance that offers good drought resistance and better tolerates light traffic.

Bahia Grass: (warm season) is low-growing, requiring less maintenance, has a coarse texture, makes a thick turf that fends off weeds.

St. Augustine Grass: (warm season) tough, vigorous, thick, weed-blocking. Tolerates some shade, but requires frequent watering, mowing and fertilizing. Standout varieties include Better Blue, Delmar, Raleigh, and Seville.

Best in hot climates

Bahia Grass: (warm season) is low-growing, requiring less maintenance, has a coarse texture, makes a thick turf that fends off weeds.

Bermuda Grass: (warm season) fine texture that tolerates traffic. Vigorous and tolerates drought and salt. Does not do well in shade and tends to build up thatch. Standout varieties include: Cheyenne, Patriot, Tifgreen, and Tifway II.

Seashore Paspalum: (warm season) tolerates sandy soil, salt, and wet conditions. Holds up to drought and tolerates traffic.

St. Augustine Grass: (warm season) tough, vigorous, thick, weed-blocking. Tolerates some shade, but requires frequent watering, mowing and fertilizing. Standout varieties include Better Blue, Delmar, Raleigh, and Seville.

Zoysiagrass: (warm season/transition zone) slow-growing, dense grass, drought tolerant. Does better with frequent

18

watering. Builds up thatch. Standout varieties include: El Toro, Emerald, and Meyer.

Best in cold climates

Fine-leaf Fescue: (cool season) does not tolerate traffic, drought resistant, shade tolerant. Some varieties are more disease resistant (Aurora)

Kentucky Bluegrass: (cool season) most common cool season grass and the hardiest for cold weather. Fine texture, fills in bare spots quickly, requires more mowing, does not do well in shady areas and does not tolerate salt. Standout varieties include Adelphi, Award, Baron, Midnight, Nu Destiny and Touchdown.

Best for drought resistance

Tall Fescue: (transition zone) low maintenance that offers good drought resistance and better tolerates light traffic. Standout varieties include Arid and Jaguar 3.

Bahia Grass: (warm season) is low-growing, requiring less maintenance, has a coarse texture, makes a thick turf that fends off weeds.

Bermuda Grass: (warm season) fine texture that tolerates traffic. Vigorous and tolerates drought and salt. Does not do well in shade and tends to build up thatch. Standout varieties include: Cheyenne, Patriot, Tifgreen, and Tifway II.

Buffalograss: (warm season) one of the few native North American grasses, is drought tolerant, but doesn't hold up to traffic. Turns brown when it gets hot and when it gets cold. Grows slowly.

Seashore Paspalum: (warm season) tolerates sandy soil, salt, and wet conditions. Holds up to drought and tolerates traffic.

Zoysiagrass: (warm season/transition zone) slow-growing, dense grass, drought tolerant. Does better with frequent watering. Builds up thatch. Standout varieties include: El Toro, Emerald, and Meyer.

Best in high-use/traffic areas

Perennial Ryegrass: (cool season and over-seeding in warm season areas) medium texture, handles traffic, handles drought conditions without a lot of additional watering or fertilizer. This grass does not do well in shade. It does mix well with other grass types.

Kentucky Bluegrass: (cool season) most common cool season grass and the hardiest for cold weather. Fine texture, fills in bare spots quickly, requires more mowing, does not do well in shady areas and does not tolerate salt. Standout varieties include Adelphi, Award, Baron, Midnight, Nu Destiny and Touchdown.

Bermuda Grass: (warm season) fine texture that tolerates traffic. Vigorous and tolerates drought and salt. Does not do well in shade and tends to build up thatch. Standout varieties include: Cheyenne, Patriot, Tifgreen, and Tifway II.

Zoysiagrass: (warm season/transition zone) slow-growing, dense grass, drought tolerant. This grass does better with frequent watering, and builds up thatch. Standout varieties include: El Toro, Emerald, and Meyer.

Best for low-maintenance requirements

Fine-leaf Fescue: (cool season) does not tolerate traffic, drought resistant, shade tolerant. Some varieties are more disease resistant (Aurora)

Tall Fescue: (transition zone) low maintenance that offers good drought resistance and better tolerates light traffic. Standout varieties include Arid and Jaguar 3.

Bahia Grass: (warm season) is low-growing, requiring less maintenance, has a coarse texture, makes a thick turf that fends off weeds.

Buffalograss: (warm season) one of the few native North American grasses, is drought tolerant, but doesn't hold up to traffic. Turns brown when it gets hot and when it gets cold. Grows slowly.

Centipedegrass: (warm season) coarse, fast-spreading, low growing and requires little fertilizer. Is not drought resistant and may turn brown in high heat. Outstanding varieties include Centennial, Oaklawn, and Tifblair.

Growing In Shady Areas

What do you do if you have a shady area that needs grass?

Well, don't fret! There are some types of grasses that are specifically designed to thrive in shaded portions of your lawn. Try a fescue in this case. However, you can still use general grass seeds as well in those shady areas, but you have to care for it properly.

Here are some suggestions:

❑ Mow at the proper height and frequency for the type of grass.

❑ Water the grass deeply.

❑ Prune or thin nearby trees to permit more sunlight to the grass.

❑ Consider mulch or shade-tolerant ground covers for densely shaded areas.

❑ If you have heavily shaded areas in your lawn where the grass is thin, consult your lawn care specialist for recommendations on improving the lawn.

To find out which of the above best-of-breed grasses will work for you contact a local lawn care professional or contact your local county extension service. They will be able to tell you through trial and error which ones will work for your situation.

You also want to be careful about mixing different species together. For example, Fine Fescue and Kentucky Bluegrass are both recommended for cold areas, but the two don't go well together in the same lawn. Fine Fescue is a bunching grass, while Kentucky Bluegrass is a spreading-type grass. You'll end up with clumps of fine fescue growing up out of your Bluegrass lawn and it will look just bad.

So, make your choice and get ready to start! How?

PLANTING THE SEED

The way you plant your grass seed depends on what shape your current lawn is in. You need to evaluate your situation and go from there!

Seeding an Existing Lawn

Let's say that you already have a lawn, but there are places that need to be filled in and thickened up. Your best bet with this type of lawn is to aerate it and over-seed.

An aerator is a machine that will poke a hole in the ground (thousands of them actually) and remove a core of soil and leave it laying on the surface. These are called core aerators. Some aerators will simply push a spike into the ground creating a hole, this type is not as good.Check with an equipment rental store to find an aerator that will work for you.

To start with, mow your grass as low as you can safely, don't throw rocks and dig dirt with the mower, but get it down to about 1" high. This will stunt the grass and slow its growth allowing the new grass that you will seed to get started with limited competition from the existing grass.

After mowing take an aerator, and go over the entire lawn at least twice. Depending on the model you use, the aerator will poke holes every 2 to 8 inches apart. If you can look down at the lawn at any point and not see spots that don't have holes larger than 6", you are doing fine. If you have a spot larger than 6" without holes in it, you won't have very much grass come up in that spot, so go over the lawn as many times as it takes to be sure you have holes everywhere.

Once you're done aerating, you will start spreading your seed, but you need to accurately measure your lawn first. Everything you do in lawn care depends on the measurement of your lawn, so do it correctly the first time and write it down so you can refer back to it whenever you need to.

The amount of seed you use is important. If you don't use enough you won't get the desired results. Most professionals will use 350 pounds per acre for lawns. Divided out per thousand square feet that is 8 pounds per thousand square feet.

Rent, buy, or borrow a seed spreader. This will make your job much easier! Do not use your hand and just throw it around, you won't get even coverage.

Spread the seed using half of the required amount spreading it in one direction, use the other half spreading the opposite direction creating a cross hatch pattern on the lawn. This way you are assured of getting even coverage.

After spreading the seed take a drag of any type, a piece of chain link fence, a board with a rope tied to it, or what ever you can drag behind your mower. Drag the lawn, this will push and drag seed into the holes you created and break up the little plugs of soil that the aerator left on the ground, it will cover up most of the seed giving much better germination and a thicker lawn.

Once you complete the dragging, spread a starter fertilizer. You can actually do this first if you want to, it really doesn't matter. A starter fertilizer has a higher middle number than first and last numbers which means more phosphate.

You will need to put down 8 pounds per thousand square feet of a 6-12-12 or 4 pounds per K of a 6-24-24. This will give the ground the nutrients needed to germinate and start a turf lawn, thus the name "starter fertilizer".

After about a month the new grass will start to yellow off some or maybe turn pale green, this is showing you that it is time to fertilize again. Apply 6# per K of 15-15-15 this will provide the nitrogen for green and growth and phosphate and potash for root growth and overall vigor.

After the grass is about 3 weeks old you should be able to start mowing. Be sure to cut it high. Fertilizing will also need to be done on a regular schedule. We'll cover these issues in later chapters.

Seeding a New Lawn

If you have a new home and this is the first lawn a few things are different. Mainly you will have to do clean up and get the proper grade before working on seeding.

Once this is done you will have to till up the ground to make a soft seed bed. After tilling fertilize, and seed just as described above using the same amount of seed. Then, cover the entire lawn with straw.

Shake out straw to cover approximately 50% of the soil from view. After done you should be able to look down and still see about half of the soil showing through the straw, no more. This equates to about 100 bales per acre.

After you're done laying down the straw it's time to start watering. Soak the lawn until runoff the first watering, followed by daily watering of sufficient length to keep the soil wet. If it dries out, the seed won't germinate.

Another option for your new lawn is to buy patches of sod. Sod can be a quick answer to aesthetic beauty, but be prepared to pay a pretty penny for this choice.

There are two integral elements of growing and maintaining a lush, green lawn. Those elements are watering and fertilizing.

WATERING YOUR LAWN

This is a very important part of lawn care. You won't have that beautiful carpet you desire in your yard if you don't give it proper watering on a regular basis. This schedule, of course, depends on the climate in which you live.

Do some research on how much rainfall your area has gotten in the past and how much is expected. The type of weather in your area will determine what type of watering system will be best for you. If you live in a dry climate, you may need an irrigation system or automatic sprinkler system.

In fact, underground automatic sprinklers are the recommended way to water lawns. When you have such a system, watering is done when it needs it on a regular basis. You won't have to mess with hoses or wasting water since all watering is done with a time.

However, these types of systems are quite costly and just may not be an option for you.

Most people will use commercial sprinklers that can be purchased quite cheaply at any discount or home store. When you use regular sprinklers, be sure to move them to different places in your yard so that the entire lawn is watered evenly. If you don't do this, you will have some spots without water and your lawn will look uneven.

Take care that you don't over water. Over watering your lawn causes more damage than a lack of water. That's because most turf grasses can handle dry spells, but not flooding.

Most grasses require 1 - 1.5" of water per week. This is enough water to moisten the soil to 4 - 6" below the surface for clay soils and 8 - 10" for sandy soils. Of course, natural rain will provide some of your watering needs.

Don't guess at how much water your lawn is getting. For measuring Mother Nature's contribution, invest in a rain gauge. If at the end of the week she's contributed enough, hold off adding more. If she comes up short, you'll want to add some supplemental watering.

Again, measure how much water your sprinkler is putting down.

You'll have to follow local regulations when there are watering bans, but just remember that less water is acceptable and grass is a very resilient plant. When the rains do return your lawn will come back with a little encouragement on your part.

As a note, you can make a type of irrigation system on your own for lawn watering by taking a simple garden hose and poking holes in it at consistent intervals. Remember, though, that you'll need to move the hose periodically to insure consistent watering.

FERTILIZERS

Your lawn consists of thousands and thousands of tiny little plants that group together closely to form patches of grass. Plants need fertilizer to grow healthy. We know we need to fertilize our garden and house plants, but often, the lawn is overlooked. A green lawn needs food to grow and thrive.

Fertilizer is any material supplying one or more essential plant nutrients. Most common turf grass fertilizers include nitrogen, phosphorous and potassium, but they may also include other essential mineral elements for turf grass growth.

Fertilizers do more than make your lawn green. They help the grass grow too, but there's a little more involved. Fertilizer will help grass seed germinate quicker and get started out of the ground. After the plants have established, fertilizer will make the grass thicker and healthier.

The most common questions asked by homeowners regarding fertilizers is how much and when. Generally speaking, most lawns will need four applications of fertilizer per year.

32

Spread fertilizing out 60 days apart starting in early spring approximately 30 days before the growing season starts in your area. Continue fertilization through the growing season until fall. Spring fertilizing gets the grass off to a fast start giving you that rich green color everyone wants.

As in watering, you should avoid using too much fertilizer.

General guidelines should be included on the bag. Too much fertilizer will cause excess growth, lead to fungus growth and weaken the grass.

What type of fertilizer should you use? Well, the answer depends on your and your needs. However, there are two basic types: complete and balanced.

Complete fertilizers contain nitrogen, phosphorous and potassium, but they may also include other essential minerals elements for turf grass growth.

Complete fertilizers contain nitrogen, phosphorous, and potassium in the same product. If a fertilizer contains less than all three elements it is referred to as an incomplete fertilizer. If urea, a 46-0-0 incomplete fertilizer, is used for every application through the season, lower turf quality may result if other essential elements are not being supplied by the soil.

Balanced fertilizers provide nutrients in a predetermined ratio that best meets the plant's requirements for those elements.

Turf grasses require nitrogen, phosphorous, and potassium in the approximate ratio of 3-1-2, 4-1-2, or 8-1-3.

Remember that the right balanced fertilizer ratio will differ with grass type, and is also influenced by soil levels of certain elements

You may want to get a slow-release fertilizer that lets their nutrients out slowly over a period of time. These fertilizers are commercially produced and available at most home stores.

Because these lawn fertilizers release their nutrients over time, rather than all at once, you're essentially stretching out the feeding. As nutrients are released, the root system of your grass fills in any bare patches. This in itself promotes lawn weed control, depriving weed seeds of a place to germinate.

Before buying these or any other lawn fertilizers, read the instructions on the bag carefully (or ask someone at the store for details). A particular product may not be suitable for your type of grass. Likewise, when applying lawn fertilizers, follow directions explicitly, concerning how much to apply, how often they should be applied, and under what conditions they should be applied.

Lawn fertilizers are best applied with spreaders. Be advised not to fill the applicator with the spreader parked on the lawn. Doing so invites grass-burn, as you may accidentally discharge too much while loading. Instead, fill the applicator somewhere else, then wheel the spreader onto the lawn.

Many people are going green with their growing using chemical free fertilizers and weed control. However, they don't necessarily provide you with an advantage when fertilizing your lawn and garden.

Plants absorb nutrients in the same way, whether the source be organic or a conventional fertilizer. Turf grass roots will only absorb dissolved nutrients found in the soil water. Organic fertilizers do not offer any advantages to the care of your lawn. The choice is strictly personal preference.

In addition, there are lawn fertilizers that promote lawn weed control at the same time. Effective lawn weed control should, after all, go hand-in-hand with the application of lawn fertilizers: if the weeds suck up some of the nutrients that you're supplying, those are nutrients being wasted, as they are not going to your grass.

Fortunately, applying lawn fertilizers and practicing weed control can be integrated into the same chore – if you play your cards right!

WEED CONTROL

Unfortunately, there's a lot more growing in your lawn than just grass. Controlling weeds in a new or existing lawn is vital to the health and overall appearance of the lawn.

A beautiful smooth lawn gets most of its good looks from the fact that it is smooth and level with no weeds sticking up above the turf. You have probably mowed your lawn before only to have dandelions popping up above the grass a day later making it look like you need to mow already.

A weed free lawn holds its good looks for several days if the grass is a monoculture with uniform growing heights.

Weeds are really just one type of plant that we have decided shouldn't be growing in one particular place. It's your point of view as to what makes a weed a weed.

Some weed-type plants are invasive and fast growing. Their growth habit overtakes our cultivated turf plants, depriving them of food and water. Other weeds are extremely noxious and cause problems for humans if they get close them.

In the lawn, the most common weeds are just a nuisance. Most don't cause skin reactions or breathing difficulties, they just don'tlook good.

What they're also telling us is that the lawn isn't as healthy as it should be. Turf grasses today are so adept at growing into thick masses, that if maintained properly, weeds are not a problem. It is when the lawn isn't as healthy as it could be that we see weeds becoming a problem for the lawn.

There are three basic types of lawn weeds:

1. Grass Type Weeds
2. Grass-Like Weeds
3. Broad Leaf Weeds

Each of these requires a different method in order to control.

Experts agree that the best way to control weeds to to prevent them from showing up in the first place. There are certain weed control products on the market right now that can accomplish this.

They are called pre-emergent controls and should ideally be applied in the spring. The soil's surface is covered with a microscopic protective layer that prevents any germinating seeds from taking hold, including crabgrass.

If left undisturbed, this protective layer will maintain its defensive qualities throughout the prime germinating period. This is when most weed seeds will normally start developing. Of course, there is no 100% guarantee that additional seeds won't be carried in by winds, birds, or any number of other methods.

Thoroughly read, understand, and follow all information on herbicide labels. Avoid windy days, as these materials can damage many landscape and garden plants if they drift (spray droplets land off the lawn). Also avoid hot days (over 85 degrees F).

It's best to have adequate soil moisture, but no rain for 24 hours after application. Don't mow for a few days before and after application. Consider spot treating weeds rather than broadcasting weed killer over the entire area.

Use caution on newly seeded areas; wait four mowings before treating newly seeded lawns and 30 days before seeding areas treated with broadleaf herbicides. Read the label regarding potential tree damage when used on lawns growing over tree root zones.

To treat for weeds in your lawn, you have to understand the type of weed that you have. Since different type weeds require different types of treatment. We'll go through some of the more common types of weeds and give you some advice how to control them.

Crabgrass

Crabgrass is the most common type of weed in lawns and it's nearly impossible to completely control this weed. Crabgrass is a warm season annual grass which grows best in the heat of midsummer when desirable lawn grasses are often semi-dormant and offer little or no competition. Crabgrass over winters as seed, comes up about mid- May or later, and is killed by the first hard frost in fall.

Crabgrass grows best in full sun. It does not grow in shady places. It will come up in clumps and look markedly different from the rest of the grass. As it grows older, it's "arms" will flop over and radiate out from the center covering the ground.

Crabgrass can be controlled in a number of ways, but the best defense against crabgrass is a thick vigorously growing lawn that is mowed no closer than 2-1/2" for cool season grasses. Use a bagger to collect grass clippings while the weed's seed heads are present.

However, you don't want to have unsightly crab grass in your lawn, so to gain control, do not apply fertilizer in summer and get a post-emergent herbicide. This type of herbicide is applied after the crabgrass has already sprouted.

Bentgrass

Bentgrass is a cool season perennial spreading grass that is commonly used for golf course greens, tees, and fairways. For the lawn owner, bentgrass is often considered a weed.

Bentgrass is not a viable option for a home lawn because it is very expensive and difficult to cultivate and care for. It is characterized as a very fine-textured, bright green grass with flat, narrow leaves.

Unfortunately, there is no herbicide you can use to get rid of bentgrass that won't damage the lawn you are meaning to grow. Patches of bentgrass will appear as fluffy, fine-textured clumps that you can remove with a spade or by just pulling.

41

When removing bentgrass, do so about 1" into the ground and re-seed.

You can try a herbicide with glyphosate to remove bentgrass, but be aware that it will kill the wanted grass along with the unwanted grass. apply the herbicide to an area about six inches or so outside the patch of Bentgrass to kill the individual stems which are creeping outwards from the patch, otherwise, these patches will reemerge.

Apply glyphosate in spring or fall when the grasses are actively growing. Wait approximately seven days, then reseed or sod the area. If you decide to till the soil prior to establishment, and see bits of Quackgrass rhizomes coming to the surface, remove these. Or wait two weeks or so until enough new Quackgrass leaves emerge and kill the new plants with a second application of glyphosate.

Dandelions

Most people are familiar with dandelions. They are a broad leaf weed that begins with bright yellow flowers that eventually change into a globe of fine filaments which are seeds that are distributed by the wind. Who hasn't blown a dandelion into the air?

42

Even though dandelions are considered a weed, they actually do have some uses in both food and medicine. They are close in character to mustard greens and are sometimes used in soups or salads.

Dandelion root is a registered drug in Canada and is used as a diuretic. It can also be used to treat anemia, jaundice, or to sooth nervousness. And, of course, who hasn't heard of dandelion wine?

If not effectively controlled, dandelions can quickly take over your yard and kill off patches of grass as they rob the soil of water and nutrients meant for the lawn. Simply picking or mowing over the flowers won't get rid of them.

Dandelions are best treated during active growing cycle with a spot treatment. If you use a dry granular form of weed killer or a weed and feed type of fertilizer, apply it to wet grass and weeds. The weed control material must stick to the leaves of the weed plants to be effective. If you spray a liquid, apply it only on a calm day so material will not drift onto desirable plants.

Remember, broadleaf weed killers are broadleaf plant killers.

They do not, for example, differentiate between dandelions and tomato plants. Apply them only to weeds in the lawn. Be careful not to get the material onto desirable plants in your yard. Read and follow all label directions.

Ground Ivy

This weed is a perennial with creeping stems that root at the nodes and has foliage that emits a mint-like odor when mowed.

Ground ivy is primarily a weed of turf grass and landscapes

Ground ivy is hard to control because you can't pull it out easily in lawns and many commercial broadleaf lawn weed killers have little or no effect on it. The most common active ingredient in granular and liquid broadleaf lawn weed killers is 2,4-D, but 2,4-D has little effect on ground ivy.

Another common active ingredient, MCPP, or, mecoprop, also has little effect on ground ivy. Dicamba is an active ingredient that does control ground ivy. Dicamba is also called Banvel.

There are several lawn weed killer products available that contain dicamba. Most of them also contain 2,4-D and MCPP. However, you may still need to make repeat applications with dicamba-containing products to completely control ground ivy. Ground ivy spreads via creeping stems that propagate new plants.

Moss

Moss in a lawn is an indication that the turf is not growing well. Moss doesn't grow in healthy lawns. Lack of fertility, soil compaction, poor drainage, shade and poor soil aeration are the most common cause of moss in lawns.

It is important to consider that moss does not kill the grass; it simply creates unfavorable growing conditions such as shade, poor drainage, poor fertility or compacted soil. These conditions, not the moss, ultimately cause the grass to die out.

If you want to eliminate moss from a lawn, focus on improving conditions for growing grass, and don't worry about the moss - t will disappear on its own as the grass gains vigor.

Herbicides and chemical control have only short term effects on moss. If herbicide use is not accompanied by proper environmental and physical controls, then the initial effect will be bare dirt or mud. Mosses will eventually return because the lawn deficiency, which led to the moss invasion, still exists.

When herbicides alone are used, the symptoms, not the cause, of a weedy lawn are being treated. Furthermore, many of the common, are ineffective against mosses, at least in some conditions. Therefore, if you perceive of the moss in your lawn as a problem, improve conditions for growing grass, rather than using herbicides.

Lime has often been suggested for moss control. Lime will raise the soil pH but will do little or nothing to prevent moss growth. The fact that the soil is acidic has little to do with the growth of moss. In fact, you can see moss growing on limestone and concrete.

48

If your lawn area is moist and shady, you will have difficulty controlling moss because you have an ideal environment for moss growth. Moss is often troublesome in spring when temperatures are cool and soil moisture high.

Mushrooms

Mushrooms, also called toadstools or puffballs, are fruiting bodies of soil fungi. They appear in lawns during wet weather in spring and summer. Mushrooms live on organic matter such as roots, stumps and boards in the soil.

Most don't harm the lawn but are unsightly. Mushrooms that grow in arcs or circles of dark green grass are called fairy rings. The arcs or rings enlarge from 3" — 2' each season as the fungi grows outward. The fairy ring fungus may interfere with water flow through the soil and stress the lawn.

There is no chemical control for mushrooms. Time is the best cure. Once the buried wood has completely decayed the mushrooms will disappear. Break mushrooms with a garden rake or lawn mower for temporary control. This helps to dry the mushrooms and reduces the risk of children eating them. Control individual mushrooms by removing the organic matter. Dig up and remove the wood. Fill and reseed, or sod, as needed.

Bermuda

Bermuda grass is an annual, fine textured "creeping grass" that grows and spreads rapidly during warm summer months. Similar to bent grass, this type of seed is commonly used on golf courses and sports fields.

Due to its rapid and sometimes widespread growth during warm months, Bermuda can quickly take over cool-season grasses while dormant. Herbicides are usually not as effective as simply hand- picking these weeds before they grow out of control.

To help prevent this, you can apply a pre-emergence just prior to its growing season (usually spring time) to prevent the seeds from germinating. However, the other extreme is to apply fluazifopbutyl or glyphosate to kill all of the grass, then reseed over it. This is only suggested if you plan on replanting or renovating your lawn afterwards.

Chickweed

Common chickweed (Stellaria media) is a matted, herbaceous, winter annual broadleaf plant. Chickweed is a prolific spring weed as it thrives under cool, wet conditions. It rarely tolerates hot, dry conditions that occur in late spring or early summer. Other common names for chickweed include starweed, winterweed, satin flower and tongue grass.

52

Chickweed is more regarded as a weed than as a useful plant, but has a place in folk medicine as a remedy for asthma, constipation, cough, fever and various other ailments. The seed of chickweed is a source of food for birds.

To remove chickweed, you'll need to hoe or hand-pull the plants. The top-growth is brittle and the roots are tenacious, so this will take some effort.

Trace the stems back to the growing point and loosen the roots - though being an annual these do not have to be completely removed, just the growing point. Dispose of uprooted plants if flowers and seed heads are present. Regular hoeing of the seedlings for a few seasons reduces the frequency of germination.

As far as weed killers you can use, a residual herbicide can be applied to suppress germination in non-cultivated areas. Look for the ingredients Paraquat or Diquat, with contact action killing top growth. Apply before flowering begins.

Dallis Grass

Dallis Grass is a broadleaf weed that closely resembles crab grass. It is one of the most difficult to control weeds for lawn care. Patches will appear in clumps with leaves that extend upright. Some patches can grow quite large if left untended and can appear unsightly in an otherwise beautiful lawn.

Dallis grass is a perennial grass with light-green color. Dallis is easily identified by its long seed-heads that protrude from the top.

Dallis tends to thrive in wet areas with lots of heat, and grows in circles out from the center of the weed.

Try to improve the drainage of your lawn to take dampness away from the areas were they grow. Additionally, allow the top of the soil to partially dry between each watering to help retain the water only in the root area.

Apply pre-emergence fertilizers (usually in the late-spring) to prevent seed germination and growth. Once weeds are established, pull them by hand and make sure you get the roots as well. After pulling, reseed the area with the desired grass.

Plantain

Broadleaf plantain is a common broadleaf weed in lawns. It is identified by oval leaf blades 2 – 6 inches long with 5 to 7 ribs that that parallel the leaf margins. In turf grass they form dense clumps

No single procedure has been successful in controlling plantain in turf grass. Early removal of new seedlings has been successful when practiced diligently.

Digging out perennial plantain plants must be done regularly for several years to be successful. Repeated applications to perennial plants with products containing 2,4-D or triclopyr can be helpful. Once these weeds are killed in open sites, these areas should be over- seeded to establish a vigorous turf grass sod.

Pre-emergent turf grass herbicides commonly used for crabgrass control have not been successful in limiting germination of plantain.

56

Isoxaben, a relatively new broadleaf pre-emergent herbicide, has been effective in limiting germination of plantain in turf grass.

Post-emergent broadleaf herbicides (2,4-D, triclopyr, MCPA, and mecoprop) can control plantain seedlings, but control of established plantain plants with post-emergent treatment is much more difficult.

For established plants, 2,4-D works best while triclopyr, MCPA, and mecoprop will only reduce its vigor. Best control is achieved from a fall application. Repeat applications are needed to kill weakened perennial weeds and new germinating seedlings.

See also removal instructions for dandelions as the removal of the two are similar.

Establishing and maintaining a healthy and beautiful lawn can be a daunting task, but if you are committed to making your home look good, it is essential that you pay attention to the quality of your lawn.

Certain types of grasses – the most commonly used, in fact – are prone to patch diseases that can devastate the most carefully groomed lawn.

PATCH DISEASES

Patch diseases will occasionally occur in bluegrass lawns. Areas of turf die in patches, hence the name. Advanced stages of the disease appear as rings of dead turf surrounding living turf that resembles a "frog's eye". Researchers have identified several fungi that cause patch-like symptoms.

Some of the more common patches include summer patch, yellow patch and necrotic ring spot.

Necrotic ring spot and yellow patch are active during cool weather in the spring and the fall, but patches may remain into the summer months. Summer patch is active during the summer period. Once established, these diseases are extremely difficult to control, and tend to occur in following years.

Red thread and pink patch are diseases that attack Kentucky bluegrass, fescues, rye grass, and bent grass. These diseases are active during the cool, moist periods of the year, causing distinct-to- irregular discolored patches to develop in lawns.

The leaves often become covered with a pink, fibrous growth. In the final stage, reddish fungal threads are found at the leaf tips. In a lawn infested with red thread or pink patch, pink areas from two to fifteen inches in diameter become readily apparent.

These spots may join to form large areas of damaged turf. Areas may turn brown and dry out. These diseases are most common under the combination of prolonged periods of high humidity, temperatures between 60?F to 75?F, and slow-growing, nitrogen-deficient turf.

To control red thread and pink patch,

❏ Mow and water correctly

❏ Maintain a sound fertilization program.

❏ For persistent problems, the lawn can be over-seeded with a more resistant turf grass variety or species.

❏ If detected soon enough, fungicides can be applied for temporary control of the disease.

Patch diseases can be very damaging to most cool-season turf grasses. These diseases cause circular patches of dead turf,

59

which may surround turf that is still green. This "frog eye" symptom often occurs with this group of diseases.

Patch diseases generally occur on sodded lawns, especially within the first 5 years of establishment. However, older lawns either established from seed or sod can also develop patch diseases.

Several fungi cause patch diseases. The actual fungal pathogen will depend on the specific patch disease. The more commonly occurring patch disease includes the following:

❑ Necrotic Ring Spot (Leptosphaeria Patch) - Leptosphaeria korrae.

❑ Summer Patch - Magnaporthe poae.

❑ Yellow Patch - Rhizoctonia cerealis.

These diseases can occur on several turf grasses, but are more damaging to Kentucky Bluegrass. In the past, some of these diseases may have been referred to as Fusarium Blight, but today are referred to by their current names.

Initial symptoms appear as small spots (2 - 4" diameter) of light green turf. Spots enlarge to form light straw colored circles, irregular patches, and crescent patterns that are 1-2 feet in diameter.

60

Centers of the patches may contain grass that is alive or dead.

When dead, the patches of grass appear crater like or sunken. Patches may overlap to form large areas of blighted turf. Symptoms may also appear as diffused patterns of yellow or brown turf. Blackening of the infected crowns, rhizomes, and roots is also characteristic. Yellow patch on bent grass generally occurs as yellow rings that often recover.

❑ Necrotic Ring Spot and Yellow Patch are favored by cool, wet conditions, occurring primarily in the spring and fall.

❑ Summer Patch is favored by hot, humid conditions and occurs in the summer.

❑ Identifying these diseases is difficult because the symptoms of Necrotic Ring Spot and Yellow Patch are still present during the summer, when Summer Patch is active.

Control of patch diseases is very difficult, and often unsuccessful. Patch diseases are more damaging if the lawn is improperly mowed and watered. Properly maintaining the turf will reduce damage and help in control.

During turf establishment, good soil preparation and selection of quality sod or seed are preventative measures. Core aeration to assist in better turf grass rooting will help in preventing disease and aid in recovery. Renovation of the diseased turf often is necessary.

Tips to help avoid patch diseases:

❑ Mow frequently at 2 1/2 to 3 inches in height.

❑ Irrigate properly.

❑ Keep thatch to a minimum.

❑ Reduce soil compaction by core aeration. (Wear golf shoes while mowing!)

❑ Fungicides generally do not provide satisfactory control of patch diseases.

Another good lawn practice is to have your lawn aerated periodically.

AERATING YOUR LAWN

The basic idea behind lawn aeration is that, like you, your lawn and the soil under it need to breathe. Providing much-needed lawn aeration for your grass entails dealing with thatch. Soils can become compacted in high-traffic areas or in areas that have mostly clay soils. This can kill off grass very quickly.

Lawn thatch is the layer of dead turf grass tissue between the green vegetation and the soil surface that must be removed (a process known as "de-thatching") to maintain lawn health. Lawn thatch is derived from stems, leaves, stolons, rhizomes and roots.

The build-up of lawn thatch makes it difficult for your lawn to breathe. Lawn aeration performed in spring or fall helps control lawn thatch. You should have your lawn aerated once a year.

The process of lawn aeration can be as simple as poking holes in the soil throughout the lawn by walking over the lawn with spiked shoes such as golf shoes. You should also faithfully remove as much lawn thatch as you can in fall by raking deeply, rather than just skimming the autumn leaves off the top of the lawn.

Lawn aeration also reduces soil compaction, allowing water and fertilizer to permeate into the root zone. Grassy areas submitted to constant foot traffic require lawn aeration more frequently.

Lawn aeration may be undertaken in the spring, as soon as the soil has thawed. But for Northern lawns, the fall season is better suited to lawn aeration. The ideal air temperature is around 60 degrees to perform lawn aeration.

If the soil is severely compacted, simple lawn aeration methods such as that mentioned above may not be sufficient. In such cases, go to a rental center and rent a piece of equipment especially for lawn aeration, called the "lawn aerator." This lawn aeration equipment will pull "cores" or plugs of soil out of the ground, letting air in.

These plugs should be 2"-3" in depth. Such a plug should be pulled out of the lawn at about every 3". The plug-removal process is facilitated by watering the lawn the day before, but don't water to the point of muddying the soil.

Likewise, if your thatch problem is severe (say, 3/4" thick or more), rent a vertical mower from a rental center. If you don't think you can do this job yourself, there's nothing wrong with hiring a lawn service to aerate your lawn.

You also need to take care of your lawn properly when it gets too long. Start with the right equipment.

CHOOSING A LAWN MOWER

You might think that lawn mowing would be a simple subject, and basically it is. However, there are some things you need to know about how to mow, when to mow, and what kind of lawn equipment you'll need.

There are all sorts of different lawn mowers on the market, you might be a little confused as to which one you should get. Well, let's see!

Reel Mowers

The type of lawn mower that has become the standard is the rotary lawn mower. But the first lawn mowers were not rotary mowers, but rather reel lawn mowers. Edwin Budding invented the reel lawn mower in 1830.

Unlike the rotary mowers you're used to, reel lawn mowers don't have an engine, relying instead merely on sharp blades and the muscle-power of the operator. Their blades also spin differently than those of a rotary mower. While a rotary mower's blades spin on a plane parallel to the ground, the blades of a reel lawn mower spin at an angle perpendicular to the ground.

The environmentally conscious extol reel lawn mowers as a pollution-free alternative to gas-powered rotary mowers. Reel lawn mowers offer many benefits in addition to being easy on the environment, including benefits in safety, noise-level, maintenance and cost.

Today's reel lawn mowers are easier to use than older models, because lightweight plastics and alloys incorporated into their construction have made them easier to maneuver.

There are, however, some drawbacks to using reel lawn mowers.

Reel lawn mowers don't chop up twigs as do rotary mowers. In fact, twigs get stuck in the blades and you'll have to remove them by hand. Nor can reel lawn mowers be used in fall to shred leaves for the compost pile.

Rotary mowers are also better at cutting tall grass, an important consideration for those who don't mow the lawn religiously. These limitations argue that, for all but the most industrious and idealistic, reel mowers may be most suitable for those who tend small urban lots.

Electric Lawn Mowers

With more and more people becoming environmentally conscious, many are turning to electric mowers for trimming their lawns.

Dragging around the cords of corded electric lawn mowers is a nuisance. It's also potentially hazardous, with the potential of accidentally running over the cord with the mower. Fortunately, electric lawn mowers are no longer synonymous with cumbersome cords.

The new cordless electric lawn mowers are safer and more flexible. An added benefit is that they start with a switch, not a pull- cord, facilitating startup. Cordless electric lawn mowers run on rechargeable batteries. Not as quiet as reel lawn mowers, cordless electric lawn mowers are still less noisy than gas-powered mowers.

Cordless mowers work best if your lawn is 1/3 of an acre or less, and if you keep your lawn mowed regularly. They're not effective for larger lawns or for tall grass, since either condition puts a lot of strain on the battery.

And pushing them up hills can put a lot of strain on the operator, so make sure you purchase a self-propelled model. Cutting moist grass also strains battery-powered mowers, although, technically, you shouldn't be mowing at all if your lawn isn't dry.

Mulching Mowers

Usually, when we hear the term, "mulching," we think of spreading mulch around by hand, using a shovel. But mulching mowers give the term, "mulching" a new twist. "Mulching" lawn mower is a bit of a misnomer. They don't make mulch; if anything, the product they leave behind is more "compost" than "mulch."

The alternative to a mulching lawn mower is a lawn mower that comes with a bag attachment to collect grass clippings. If you opt for the latter, you should deposit the clippings into a compost pile, so as to acquire free compost for the garden and avoid wasting community landfill space.

The grass clippings left behind by a mulching mower essentially function as a lawn fertilizer, as if you were applying compost to the lawn. For this reason, it makes more sense for most urban and suburban homeowners to use a mulching mower, rather than bagging their grass clippings and dumping them in the compost pile.

Essentially, mulching lawn mowers eliminate the "middleman," namely, the compost pile, instead providing you with compost directly. This means less work for you.

Mulching lawn mowers are designed so as to leave behind finely shredded grass clippings. Such clippings can be left on the lawn with impunity. By contrast, because lawn mowers without mulching capabilities produce clippings that are bulkier and readily mat together, their clippings need to be removed from the lawn, so that the grass doesn't suffocate under them.

Rotary Mowers

What's best will depend on your wants and needs. Gas-powered rotary lawn mowers can be divided into two categories: walk-behind rotary mowers and riding mowers / lawn tractors.

The walk-behind rotary lawn mowers can further be classified according to whether they're push-type lawn mowers or self-propelled. Purchase price varies greatly between these types of rotary lawn mowers, with riding mowers / lawn tractors being the most expensive, followed by self-propelled mowers.

The push-type mowers are the least expensive because they require you to provide the muscle to make them move.

Self-propelled rotary lawn mowers require the operator to squeeze a bar to engage the mower, which causes the machine to take off -- all you have to do is control the direction in which it goes. If you release your grip on the bar, the mower blade stops spinning.

For the higher-end self-propelled rotary mowers, the drive system does not shut off when you release the bar – a convenient feature, in case you'd like to transport the lawn mower from point A to point B without cutting grass along the way.

The difference between riding lawn mowers and lawn tractors lies in the location of the cutting deck. Lawn tractors have a mid- mounted cutting deck, while for riding lawn mowers the cutting deck is located under the front of the vehicle. The front-end location of the cutting deck on riding lawn mowers makes these machines more maneuverable. Maneuverability becomes an issue when, for instance, a lawn is dotted with shrubs and trees.

With both riding lawn mowers and lawn tractors you can make use of accessories ranging from brushes for spring cleaning to snow- removal attachments.

As with all lawn mowers, caution must be exercised when operating riding lawn mowers and lawn tractors. While providing them with a "vehicle" may seem like a great way to get the kids to mow the lawn without complaining, only those mature enough to handle heavy equipment should be allowed to operate riding lawn mowers and lawn tractors.

Choose a mower that's in your price range that meets the needs and standards that you have assigned to it. Go for comfort, though – in the long run, you'll be glad you did!

Now that you've got the equipment, you're ready to put it to ork!

MOWING THE LAWN

Proper mowing, along with proper watering, can be the most critical factor in the appearance of a lawn. Good mowing techniques not only enhance the appearance of the lawn, but also increase the turf grass vigor.

There actually is a right and wrong time to mow. Most people just look at their lawns and decide if it's long enough to warrant a mowing, but you are going for that professionally landscaped look, so you need to pay heed to the expert's advice.

Lawn mowing should not be done when the grass is wet (under which conditions disease can be introduced, plus you incur the risk of slipping and getting injured).

Also, lawn mowing in the evening puts less stress on the lawn than lawn mowing when the sun is pounding down in the afternoon. Mowing during the heat of the day during hot weather may cause the lawn to brown. It is best to mow during the cooler part of the day.

Mowing frequency will change throughout the year with different weather patterns. Cool season grasses such as Kentucky bluegrass may require mowing twice a week in the spring, but only every 7-10 days in the summer. Warm season grasses such as Bermuda grass may need more frequent mowing in the summer than in the fall or spring.

Aesthetics aside, there's a good lawn-care reason not to wait longer in between mowing, each time simply mowing the lawn when the grass is higher and reducing the overall number of mowing. Sure, such a policy would reduce time spent on lawn care. But you get out of lawn care what you put into it.

It may come as a surprise that mowing the lawn is about more than just keeping your lawn's height under control. If done properly, mowing stimulates the grass of your lawn to lushness and better health, just as pinching a garden plant can improve its appearance. Proper mowing technique is an important aspect of overall lawn care.

So what is a proper mowing technique? Generally, you should alternate the direction in which you mow each lawn mowing session. You will thereby prevent your grass from "getting into a rut" (literally).

If your lawn mower wheels pass over the same area in the same direction each time you mow, they'll form ruts over time.

Switching lawn mowing patterns also wisely avoids having the lawn mower blade beating at the grass in the same direction at every mowing.

Novices will just set the mower at the lowest setting to cut the grass as close to the ground as possible thus cutting down on the frequency of needing to mow. This isn't a good practice.

Certain grasses need to mown to a certain height to promote growth and healthiness. A general rule of thumb for almost all grasses is to mow to between 2 and 3 inches in height.

Height is important because the grass uses the extra length to absorb the sunshine it needs to grow and develop into a healthy plant. Never remove more than 1/3 at any one mowing. This may mean you'll have to mow more often during prime growing times (usually spring and early fall).

Turf grass stressed by mowing too low is more prone to disease, weed invasion, drought and traffic stress. Removal of most of the leaf blade limits food production. Limited food production decreases root, thizome, and stolon growth. Plants with limited food production and a limited root system will not have vigorous growth.

A vigorous, dense turf grass area is one of the best defenses against weed invasion. Weak grass plants with a limited root system are more prone to drought damage. It is

75

particularly important to mow high during dry weather. Mowing height varies for different turf grass species:

Many turf grasses such as Kentucky bluegrass should be cut at 2 1/2 to 3 inches. Bentgrass and bermuda grass should be cut at 1 to 1 1/2 inches. Determine the type of turf grass in a lawn before recommending mowing heights. The grass should be mowed so that no more than 1/3 of the leaf blade is removed. If the desired height is 3", mow the grass when it has grown to 4".

If you let the grass grow too long and then mow it too low, scalping will occur on your lawn. When you do this, excess leaf blade tissue is removed. Such "scalping" of the lawn can cause severe visual damage.

More importantly, scalping shocks the grass plants and growth slows or stops, limiting the vigor of the turf. A scalped lawn may dry out quickly from drought, or may develop unusual weed and disease problems.

You will also want to make sure your mower blades are sharp. A dull mower blade shreds the tips of the grass blades. The shredding opens the ends of the leaf blades for increased moisture loss and potentially provides a site for disease invasion. Lawns cut with a dull mower blade may have an overall white appearance from the shredded grass blades.

76

If your lawn isn't looking the way you envisioned it, take a good look at how it is being mown. You'll need to revise your mowing practices if any of the following is present:

- Frayed grass blades
- Excess clumps of clippings
- Tall grass mowed short resulting in a yellow color
- Short grass with thin areas and weeds

So, that's about it for mowing. However, you're still left with all those clippings after you're done. What do you with all that?

GRASS CLIPPINGS – KEEP OR TOSS

There are two schools of thought when it comes to this issue – neither of which is definitive.

Some people say leave the clippings on the lawn after you mow.

This not only saves time and energy, but the clippings decompose quickly and add vital nutrients back into the soil.

In fact, recycling grass clippings has recently taken on a movement of its own. Proponents call this practice "grass-cycling" and advocate that leaving those clipping where they lay saves time, landfill space and nurtures the soil.

The Professional Lawn Care Association says that About 20 percent of all waste that goes into a landfill is landscape debris and about half of that is simply grass clippings. With yard waste bans in place in many areas of the country, "grass-cycling" offers you an alternative, and at the same time increases the health and beauty of your lawn.

78

Grass clippings are 85 percent water, decompose rapidly, and return nutrients to the soil with no thatch buildup. They actually return 20 percent of their nitrogen to the soil to feed the lawn's root system. And grass-cycling can be practiced year-round with most mowers.

On the other side of the spectrum, others say that leaving clippings on your lawn is not only unsightly, but it can cause damage to your lawn as well. Leaving grass clippings on the lawn becomes a problem only if they are too thick. If you mow the lawn before it gets overly tall, the mass of the grass clippings will not be sufficient to warrant raking.

When cut grass lays in large clumps, it could be preventing the grass below it from getting the sunshine and water that it needs to grow. This could leave behind unsightly brown patches of dead grass.

A good way to obviate having to rake grass clippings is to mow with mulching lawn mowers. When you have a mulching mower, the clippings are gathered in a bag and can be used in compost piles for fertilization.

Using mulching mowers can not only cut down on your yard maintenance, but also makes your grass greener. Otherwise, you may end up either raking or bagging your grass clippings -- which in turn mean disposing of those grass clippings or recycling them - all of which means extra work.

The bottom line is that as long as you are mowing on a regular basis and you don't leave behind clumps of clippings, it won't cause any harm leaving those clipping right where they are.

What about the leaves that cover your lawn in the fall?

LEAF REMOVAL

Fall leaf removal is not only necessary from an aesthetic perspective but also from an agronomic perspective. Although turf grass growth slows or ceases this time of the year, the plant will continue to photosynthesize as long as the turf is green.

Energy in the form of carbohydrates captured and stored from photosynthesis will go to enhance root growth and accumulate in the storage compartments (nodes, crowns, etc) to be used the following year. Leaves left on the turf grass shade the turf grass leaves reducing the turf plants ability to photosynthesize.

Thus, the full potential to capture sunlight is greatly diminished when leaves are left on the turf. Additionally, if the leaves get wet, a microclimate under these leaves promote disease development.

The primary diseases that are favored by this environment are (also known as pink snow mold or fusarium patch) and powdery mildew. Thus, blowing or raking those leaves off the turf is an important fall agronomic practice.

Owning and taking care of a lawn mower is similar to owning and taking care of a car. If it is neglected, performance will suffer.

CARING FOR YOUR MOWER

It doesn't matter that you've neglected your lawn mower well into the season. Start caring for it now! First, install fresh spark plugs. They're inexpensive enough to replace rather than clean or gap.

If your mower has a paper air filter, give that a complete replacement, too. For foam air filters, buy new mower replacement foam and soak it oil before installing.

Dull blades harm lawns. Ripped out chunks of grass are highly vulnerable to a myriad of lawn diseases. Either remove the blade with a socket wrench, hone it with a file (following the existing cutting angle), or take it to a lawn-care shop for professional sharpening.

It's just good sense before doing any of this work to run the mower until it runs completely out of gas. Turn the mower filter-side up (to prevent clogging) and drain the oil. Be sure to remove the plug or plug wire to keep the mower from firing up while you're up to your elbows in machinery.

Be sure the tires are fully inflated – especially with riding mowers. Under-inflated tires on a riding mower can cause what we, in our family, usually refer to as crop circles – unevenly mowed patches that resemble that otherworld phenomenon that some people think exist.

Tuning Up Your Mower

At the beginning of the mowing season, you should ideally perform a tune-up on your machine. What does that entail? Here's a step-by-step guide:

1. Warm up the engine. Put just enough gas in the gas tank to get your lawn mower running. Start your engine and let it run until it runs out of gas.

2. Disconnect the spark plug wire so that the engine can't start accidentally.

3. Change the oil using the following procedure:

a. e sure you purchase the right type of oil for your replacement oil.

b. an off any dirt around the upper part of the oil tank (where you fill your machine with oil). An old toothbrush comes in handy for this task. Unscrew and remove the dipstick, if your oil tank has one.

c. locate the lower side of your oil tank – a plug found on the underside of your machine. You need to drain out the old oil, and unscrewing this plug will do just that.

Prop up your machine accordingly with blocks, providing a tilt that will give you access to the plug. Stick an oil pan or like container under the plug to catch the oil. Ready?

Okay, unscrew the plug (you may need a socket wrench) by turning counter-clockwise and let that dirty oil pour out. And I do mean dirty: obviously, you don't want to have your "Sunday best" on when performing a lawn mower tune-up!

a. Screw the drain plug back on using a clockwise motion. Don't over-tighten; so that you'll be able to get it off easily next time you need a lawn mower tune-up.

Rather than over-tightening when you work on your machine, it's better to tighten moderately, and then periodically check during the mowing season to ensure that it hasn't loosened through vibrations.

b. If your machine has an oil filter, replace it as part of the lawn mower tune-up and clean the gasket with which it comes into contact.

c. Remove the blocks so that your machine is level again.

d. Fill the oil tank with new oil to the correct level, replacing cap and dipstick.

e. Refill lawn mower with gas and reconnect spark plug wire.

f. At this point in the lawn mower tune-up, it's time to start the machine. Let the engine idle and ensure that there are no oil leaks.

4. Change the spark plugs as follows:

a. Clean the housing around the old spark plug.

b. Remove the old spark plug with socket wrench.

c. Unfortunately, at this point you'll have to check the blasted manual again (don't you just hate that?) What you need to do is ensure that the new spark plug is gapped the way it's supposed to be for your machine.

Just measure the gap and see if the measurement matches the manufacturer's specifications for your machine. If it doesn't match (or if there's no gap at all), you'll have to create/alter the gap.

d. Screw on the new spark plug (not too tight!).

5. Figure out what type of air filter you have: paper or foam. Paper will be replaced, foam will be cleaned

Changing a Paper Filter:

a. Unscrew the cover and remove the paper air filter.

b. Insert a new filter with the pleat facing out

c. Screw the cover back on.

Cleaning a Foam Filter:

a. Unscrew the cover

b. Remove the air filter unit and discard the old foam.

c. Clean the air filter unit with kerosene.

d. Soak the new piece of foam in clean engine oil. Squeeze out excess oil using a clean rag.

e. Insert new foam in air filter. Ensure the lip protrudes over the edge of the unit.

f. Screw the cover back on.

6. Connect the new spark plug and VOILA! You're done!

Winterizing Your Mower

You should also take precautions at the end of the season to properly winterize your mower if you live in an area where cold weather is a problem.

Preparing a lawn mower for winter storage is easy to do with 7 simple steps. Not only will proper winterizing save you money and frustration, winter maintenance will also reduce emissions next spring. A lawn mower in good working condition is both safer and better for your lawn.

Winterizing mowers takes several steps, including draining the gas, cleaning the mower, replacing air filters, and changing the oil. When not properly maintained, lawn mowers can not only be frustrating and costly but also damaging to the environment and unsafe. Older mowers, especially those that haven't been properly maintained, do not perform as well and may be dangerous.

Following these easy maintenance steps for your lawn mower this winter will save you time and frustration with lawn mower repairs next spring:

- Drain the gas out of the tank
- Clean the undercarriage with a brush and hot soapy water, making sure to rinse well
- Sharpen the blade and spray it with a light coating of WD40
- Replace the air filter
- Change the oil
- With the spark plug removed, apply a drop of oil into the sparkplug hole
- Lube the cables and throttle control
- Store your mower in a sheltered area

Next year, always check the undercarriage and in the discharge chute and bag for critters that may have decided to use your lawn mower as a winter get-away. It'll save both you and the critters from a lot of discomfort.

This book is about lawn care, but part of having a beautiful lawn is having an aesthetically pleasing look in front of your house. In the next section, we'll give you some tips on landscaping to enhance your lawn.

LANDSCAPING

Because you're a homeowner, you want to take a certain pride in how other people view your home. It's your castle, your haven, and your property. You want it to look as good as it can when people pass by. A great lawn is just a start. You should also include landscaping along with your lush green lawn to improve the beauty of your home's outside.

Landscaping also will raise your property values markedly.

According to many realtors, adding landscaping effects can increase the value of your home and property by as much as fifteen percent!

You don't have to go hog wild with your landscaping. And, it doesn't have to cost a lot of money. We have some great ideas for you to try!

The first aspect of landscaping you should address is any existing trees that are in your yard. Take a good look at those trees noticing any unsightly limbs or limbs that are looming over your home. These limbs need to come off not only for looks but for safety as well.

You can do this yourself with a long-arm tree trimmer or hire a tree service. You'll be surprised at what an improvement a little tree trimming can be!

Go to your local nursery or home improvement store and browse through their plants to see which ones appeal to you. Don't just look at flowers, notice trees and bushes as well. Take note of their cost and names as well as the care that will be required for these plants.

You'll want to include a mix of shrubs, plants, and flowers to make your landscaping interesting and pleasant to look at. Here are some of the more popular choices among homeowners:

Azaleas

Azaleas are flowering bushes that come in many colors. When in full bloom, these bushes are striking in their beauty. They need to be planted in a partially shaded area. If you put your azalea bush in full sun, you'll need to make sure it has plenty of water.

Butterfly Bush

The best part about this plant is that they will attract all sorts of butterflies to your yard further improving the beauty you are offering those around you! They come in blooms of purple, pink, white, or red and can get as tall as 6 to 12 feet! These bushes adapt best to full sun.

Roses

So many people love beautiful roses, it's a good compliment to your gorgeous green lawn. Color choices are vast and varied as are the types of bushes you can buy. Some can grow quite tall while others can remain smaller. Roses can require a lot of attention and care, but the results are amazingly satisfying. They need about six hours of full sun per day.

Common English Boxwood Shrub

This is a very common shrub used in yard all over the world. They have densely packed green leaves and are rounded in shape. They can be shaped easily with shrub trimmers. They should be planted in partial shade.

Yews

Yew shrubs can be large or small depending on the variety. They are needle-bearing evergreens in a deep green color on top which is lighter underneath. Yews can grow in sun or shade.

Winterberry Holly

This bush is a fun little eye catcher that stays beautiful all through the winter. They have small, white flowers in the spring and produce bright red berries that remain into the winter. It can be grown in full sun or partial shade, and will attract songbirds to your yard! What a wonderful perk!

Sumac

The sumac is a tree that gives a beautiful performance in the fall when the leaves change color. There are many varieties, but stay away from the poison sumac! They need full sun to partial shade.

Hydrangea

Hydrangea bushes are just beautiful additions to any yard. They have bright green leaves and huge, round flowers in a variety of colors. They can grow in partial shade.

Spirea

The spirea shrub reaches a height of 2-3' and spreads out 2-3'. It requires full sun. The shrub's foliage is dark green in summer, but its fall color is red. In May the plant bears small, white flowers in clusters.

100

Forsythia

These early bloomers sport the vibrant yellow flowers that have become a fixture of spring dreams. Their flowers precede their leaves. There are different varieties that grow in different ways, so do your research. They grow best in full sun.

There are many varieties of trees that can make your yard a real showplace as well. When you buy a tree, however, remember that you will have to wait a few years before you can enjoy the beauty it has to offer. Consider these varieties.

Magnolia Tree

Dogwood Tree

102

Plum Tree

Japanese Maple

Birch Tree

There are also hundreds of types of flowers that you can plant in beds throughout your yard. Some are annuals, but your best bet is to go for perennials so you can watch the flowers come up year after year without having to plant them!

Once you've taken a good look around the nursery, don't buy anything yet! Go home and look at your yard. Think of the best places to put the plants you like to achieve an eye-catching display.

Sit down with a piece of paper and map out your yard. Be sure to check with the utility companies (power, cable, etc.) to find out if and where there are any buried wires. Make note of where you want certain plants, bushes, and trees to go. Group

104

together those plants that share the same care and light considerations.

Then go wild – well within your budget that is. Buy your plants and trees and install them in your yard.

For bushes and trees, you'll need to dig a large hole that can fully accommodate the root ball. Once your tree or bush is in the ground, mulch around it and apply some fertilizer. After that's done, just water and you're done.

Pay close attention to these plants while they are acclimating themselves to the ground and spreading their roots to take hold.

Fertilize and water on a regular basis then enjoy your new plants.

Landscaping is about more than just pretty plants, bushes, trees, and flowers. There are also some other aspects you can add to make your yard pleasant and beautiful.

Building a deck or porch onto your home is a great way to not only increase outdoor space for lounging on cool spring nights, but also to add an interesting focal point. You can easily build your own deck with a little carpentry know-how. Many home improvement stores carry deck plans and can even help you with all the supplies you'll need.

Another very interesting addition to a yard is a rock waterfall.

BUILDING A WATERFALL

You can easily build your own water garden to add interest to your yard. The process isn't very difficult and can be achieved with little expense. We're big fans of the waterfall garden, so here's a step- by-step guide to building your own waterfall right in your own yard!

First, gather your supplies. Most of these can be found at hardware stores or discount home stores like Lowe's or Home Depot. Here's what you'll need:

- 25-30 rocks of various sizes. Try to get some large flat ones too.
- Submersible pump.
- Tubing to run from pump to top of waterfall.
- Large plastic flower pot (or similar) to house tubing.
- Rigid pond liner.
- Carpenter's level.

- Shovel.
- Sand.
- Garden hose.

Your waterfall will run on electricity, so it will need to have its own outlet for a power source. Ideally, the construction of a waterfall should be done by a patio, deck, or porch. If you don't have an outdoor outlet, one will have to be installed by a certified electrician.

Remove all weeds in the area where you will be digging for your pond. Make sure the area is level. Measure the liner you have chosen so you can dig a hole big enough to hold it. Simply invert the liner and trace around it on the ground. Then start digging!

The depth of the hole should be the same depth as the liner and the diameter as close to the actual diameter of the liner as possible to insure a nice, snug fit. If you find your hole is a little bigger than the liner, just fill in the sides with sand.

Sand will also be used at the bottom of the hole, since sand floors provide the stability needed to play with the height of preformed liners. Put about an inch of sand in, so that the top rim of the preformed liner will stand about an inch above ground level -- reducing the amount of dirt that will keep falling into your waterfall pond. You'll be pushing the sand around to get the level of the preformed liner just right.

Next, place the preformed liner into the hole for the waterfall pond. Check for levelness by placing a carpenter's level across it -- both front to back and left to right. Depending on the readings you get from the carpenter's level, it is at this point that you'll have to remove the preformed liner from the hole and adjust its sandy floor accordingly.

OK, prep work is out of the way, it's time to move on to the structure itself.

Take a look at the rocks you have. The most important rocks are what might be termed the "spillway" rocks. The spillway rocks are the ones directly over which the water will cascade.

The spillway rocks should be relatively flat as opposed to rocks that are more rounded in shape. They should also have sharp, squared edges. Water will cascade more cleanly over such edges. When rocks have blunt, gently-curving edges, some of the water tends to follow that curve and trickle back under the rocks.

The idea behind the selection of spillway rocks for a cascade design is to choose rocks that are most likely to channel the falling water in the precise direction in which you want it to
108

go. How you lay the spillway rocks is also important to this end, as you'll see later.

In addition to seeking out relatively flat rocks with sharp edges, see if you can't find rocks that are slightly cupped. That is, occasionally you'll come across rocks that curl up ever so slightly at the edges, leaving a depression in the middle. The natural channel in such rocks will be greatly advantageous for the creation of the spillways in your cascade design. Their raised edges will help keep the water from deviating where you don't want it namely, behind the rocks.

You'll essentially be building four mini-rock walls around the pot, to box it in. Make a small trench for the tubing to sit in under the rocks, so that the rocks don't weigh it down. This will keep the tubing free, so that you can slide it through the pot up or down, at will. This gives you the leeway that you need, since you won't know at exactly what height you'll want the water spouting out until you've finished laying the rocks.

You may have been wondering what the flower pot in the supply list is for. You'll need a pot about 11" high with a drainage hole in the bottom that matches the diameter of your tubing. The pot functions as housing for the tubing within the cascading structure for the waterfall. You could easily substitute something else that might work better and can use either a terra cotta or plastic variety. The idea is to have some sort of housing to hold the tubing in place, while you lay up the rocks all around it. This housing won't show when you're finished: it will lie hidden at the center of your rock work.

After laying a first course of rocks in the front, cover them with a sheet of black plastic. Extend one end of the plastic up to the top of the plastic pot, while tucking the other over the lip of the preformed pond liner and down into the water. Then disguise the plastic with rocks, so that it wouldn't be visible in the pond. The plastic serves the purpose of catching more water than the rocks alone could and funnel it into the pond. Much of the water that would otherwise be lost to splashing strikes against this plastic and falls back into the pond, instead.

Also after laying the first course of rocks in front and just after laying the black plastic, lay one long, flat rock spanning them all and sitting right on top of that plastic. The long, flat rock juts out in the direction of the pond, forming an overhang. It will serve as a shelf for your first spillway rock, so it will be referred to as the "shelf rock."

Invert the flower pot and thread your tubing through the hole in its bottom. Place the pot on the ground (still inverted) at the center of what will be the rock waterfall structure. How far in back of the pond should this be? Well, that depends on the
110

depth of your rocks. You'll want the rocks that face the pond to abut it; if possible, they should even overhang the pond slightly. So if the rocks you'll be using there are 8" in depth (i.e., front to back), the front side of the pot should be about 8" back from the edge of the pond.

How long should the tubing be? Leave yourself with a length that is longer than what you'll need, and trim later as necessary. This will make your job a lot easier! As to where to run it along the ground, choose either the left or the right side of the pond and rock waterfall. As a cosmetic touch at the end of the project, you can go back and hide it with stones and/or mulch.

Typically, when building rock walls, it's a good idea to stagger the seams. Of course, these will be very small rock walls, so it's not a structural concern here. Still, try to do some staggering, if only because it looks better.

As already mentioned in speaking of rock selection, after the first course of rocks in the front was down, you put one long flat rock spanning them all. Why? Because this rock's function is to form an overhang, it's a key piece in your cascade design. Using it as a shelf, you'll place your first spillway rock on it, in such a way that the spillway rock overhangs the pond even further.

Continue laying the 4 walls, until you've reached the height you desire. Once you're done encasing the pot with the 4 walls, you need to place 2 longer stones across the top (either front-to-back or left-to- right) to span the walls. Pull up the tubing to gain more length, if necessary, and gently sandwich the tubing in between these 2 longer rocks to hold it in place.

Begin trying to position your first spillway rock on top of your shelf rock. It should jut out over the pond even further than does the shelf rock. Ideally, the tip would line up over the middle of the pond, although this is difficult to achieve. Elevate the first spillway rock in the back, to achieve better water run-off. You can elevate this or any rock in the wall by using shims in small flat stones.

Bend the end of the tubing down towards the pond and place one or more capstones over it. It is under here that the waterfall's "spout" will rest, so to speak. By "capstone" I mean a stone that will partially hide the tubing and/or gently press it down against the second spillway rock. Make sure most of the capstone's weight rests on the rocks between which the tubing is sandwiched or on shims, so that the tubing doesn't become flattened. You'll have to play with the level of the spout, as you begin to fit in the second spillway rock.

112

Begin trying to position your second spillway rock on top of your first spillway rock. Again, elevate the rock in the back using a shim, to achieve a steeper pitch. One way to think of the placement of the 2 spillway rocks is that they're like 2 shingles on a roof. They're both on a slant, and the top one overlaps the bottom one, forming a continuous chute down which the water can pour.

The position of the end of the tubing that forms the spout can now be determined more precisely, as you size it up on the surface of the second spillway rock. Again, pull to lengthen or shorten your tubing, as necessary.

You're ready to fill the pond with water, plug in the pump's cord, and test the flow of your natural rock waterfall. No doubt, you'll have to make several adjustments before you get everything right. The objective is to get the water to fall as close as possible to the middle of the pond, so that you can minimize water-loss from the splashing that will incur.

There is some compromise involved with your cascade design: greater height equals greater visual impact, but greater height also equals greater water-loss as the splashes will be more violent. Another consideration on height: keep your natural rock waterfall in proportion with the pond. A general rule of thumb would be, the smaller the pond, the shorter the rock waterfall.

The entire structure is built with the intent to minimize water loss, but regardless of how well you do at minimizing water-loss, it is prudent to check the level of your waterfall pond water periodically. Should the pond go dry due to water-loss, you'll burn out the pump.

Consequently, you must turn off the pump overnight or when leaving your property. Of course, if you're frugal, you'll unplug the pump when you're not around anyhow, to save money on electricity. Since this water feature is intended only for decoration and for relaxation (it's not a fish pool), there's no reason to keep it running if you're not there to enjoy it.

CONCLUSION

Having a beautiful lawn is more beneficial than the aesthetic feeling of your home.

Acting like a gigantic sponge, lawns absorb all types of airborne pollutants such as soot, dust and carbon dioxide, as well as noise. Less weeds mean less weed pollen, a relief of those with allergies.

Lawns help to improve water quality. Water quality gets a boost from a common plant we see everyday-the grass plant. According to experts, a well-managed lawn helps prevent runoff and is a natural water fiber.

A healthy turf can help prevent runoff and soil erosion. In fact, turf promotes high populations of microorganisms in the thatch layer and topsoil. These microorganisms break down impurities making turf an excellent water filter.

Healthy lawns can have a cooling effect on your entire neighborhood! The front lawns of a block of eight average houses have the cooling effect of about 70 tons of air conditioning-enough to cool 16 average houses.

On a hot summer day, grass can be 10-14 degrees cooler than exposed soil and as much as 30 degrees cooler than concrete or asphalt. And it also provides oxygen. A 50' x 50' well-maintained grass area will create enough oxygen to meet the needs of a family of four every day.

A good lawn also increases property value. A great lawn has more than just health value. Appraisers estimate that a well-landscaped and maintained lawn adds 7% to the value of residential property. A recent Gallup Survey concluded that a 15% increase in selling price can be realized when the home is nicely landscaped.

Your lawn is your own little piece of the world – one that you can make as beautiful as your mind can imagine. A beautiful, green lawn can be so satisfying to the homeowner. Take all the steps in this book to insure that your little piece of the world makes you happy!

9 786069 838075

Printed by Libri Plureos GmbH in Hamburg, Germany